UNHEALTHY RELATIONSHIP HABITS

15 Practices for Couples to Steer a Toxic Relationship into A More Loving, Relaxed, Happy, Close and Enjoying Relationship Starting from Today!

Contents

<u>INTRODUCTION</u>
<u>CHAPTER 1</u>
<u>CHAPTER 2</u>
<u>CHAPTER 3</u>
<u>CHAPTER 4</u>
<u>CHAPTER 5</u>
<u>CHAPTER 6</u>
<u>CHAPTER 7</u>
<u>CHAPTER 8</u>
<u>CHAPTER 9</u>
<u>CHAPTER 10</u>
<u>CONCLUSION</u>

INTRODUCTION

Most relationships start out with the best of intentions. Couples are happy, in love, and ready to take on the world together. However, some unhealthy relationship habits can develop over time that can lead to a toxic relationship.

Couples aware of these practices can take steps to break the cycle and build a healthier, happier relationship together.

If you are currently in a toxic relationship or want to avoid one, read on for **15 practices to help you have a more loving and relaxed relationship starting today!**

CHAPTER 1

WHAT MAKES A RELATIONSHIP HEALTHY?

OR UNHEALTHY?

Unhealthy relationship habits are not just the things you do but also your thoughts about your partner. These habits can be detrimental to relationships and often lead to breakups. The following unhealthy relationship habits may be some of those that are hurting your relationship right now. But don't worry! There is hope for a healthier future with some changes.

UNHEALTHY RELATIONSHIP HABITS:

- *Comparing your partner to others.*
- *Instead of focusing on the positive, people tend to focus on the negative.*
- *Accusing your partner for everything that goes wrong in your life.*
- *Ignoring your partner's feelings and needs.*
- *Making assumptions about your partner's feelings or thoughts. Criticizing your partner constantly.*
- *Sabotaging your partner's efforts.*
- *As a kind of punishment, withholding love and affection.*
- *Refusing to apologize or take responsibility for your actions.*
- *Acting entitled and demanding.*
- *Trying to change your partner instead of accepting them for who they are.*
- *Engaging in mind-reading games.*
- *Holding grudges and refusing to forgive.*
- *Using your partner as a punching bag.*
- *Taking your partner for granted.*

HOW TO CHANGE UNHEALTHY RELATIONSHIP HABITS

The best way to help your relationship is by being a better partner.
You need to be aware of the toxic habits that are hurting your relationship and then make an effort to change them. It's not easy, but if you want a healthy, happy long-term partnership, it's something you'll need to do.

Here are a few tips for changing your unhealthy relationship habits:

Begin by admitting to yourself that you have a problem.
Be honest with yourself and your partner about what you need to change.
Commit to change your behavior and follow through on it.
Ask your partner for their help and support in changing your habits.
Celebrate every success, no matter how small. How to deal with a partner who has unhealthy relationship habits It can be hard when you're dealing with an unhappy or toxic relationship, but there are some things You can do the following things to make yourself feel better about the situation: Recognize that you are not responsible for your partner's behavior.
The most important thing is to look for yourself physically and mentally. Talk to someone who can help you process what's going on in your relationship.
Find ways to express your feelings that don't involve your partner.
Remove yourself from any situations that are harmful or toxic.
Remember that it's not your fault and you can't change your partner.

The most important thing is to lookout for yourself physically and mentally. It's not easy to do, but it's worth it in the long run. You deserve a healthy, happy relationship with someone who loves and respects you.

CHAPTER 2

TOXIC BEHAVIORS THAT CAN TEAR COUPLES APART

The signs of a toxic relationship are more than just fighting, they can also come in the form of toxic habits. These behaviors are designed to tear couples apart by making them feel shame, fear, anger and sadness. Toxic habits can change one's mind about their partner and make them not want to be with that person or make it difficult to fall in love again.

Many of these habits are not inherent to the person, but they can be learned. It's important to understand that your partner may have some bad habits or behaviors that you can change and replace with positive ones. Here is a list of the top eight toxic relationship habits that are tearing couples apart today:

Neglecting your partner: This is a toxic behavior where one person in the relationship intentionally ignores their partner. They may not return calls, texts, or emails and may even avoid seeing them altogether. This can leave the other person feeling neglected and unimportant, leading to more resentment down the road.

Triangulation: Triangulation is a toxic habit where one person will go to other people for support instead of their partner. This can leave the partner feeling left out and unimportant. It can also lead to disagreements between all three people involved.

Lack of communication: Lack of communication is another big problem in relationships. When couples stop talking to each other, they stop understanding each other. This can lead to a lot of built-up resentment and anger.

Criticism: Criticism is another toxic habit that can destroy relationships. When one partner constantly criticizes the other, it makes them feel bad about themselves and eventually resentment.

Controlling behavior: A controlling partner will try to manipulate their partner into doing what they want. This might cause the other person to feel trapped and smothered, which can be highly destructive to a relationship. Blame: Blaming your partner for everything wrong in the relationship is a toxic habit that will only lead to more fights. It's important to take responsibility for your own actions and not place all the blame on someone else.

Stonewalling: Stonewalling is another toxic habit that can destroy a relationship. This happens when one person puts up an emotional wall between themselves and their partner, refusing to have any kind of communication with them at all times. It often leads to the other person feeling rejected or not important enough for their needs to matter.

Lack of empathy: Lack of empathy is another toxic habit that can destroy relationships. This happens when one person doesn't care about their partner's feelings and only thinks about themselves. The other person feels like they're not important enough to be heard or listened to by the other person in the relationship, leading them down a path towards resentment.

If you're struggling with any of these toxic habits, it's important to address them head-on and work towards changing them. Couples therapy can be a great way to help identify and change these behaviors so that you can have a healthy, happy relationship!

CHAPTER 3

QUESTIONS THAT WILL SAVE YOUR RELATIONSHIP

It's not always easy to spot when a relationship is in trouble. Sometimes, we may be so used to arguing and bickering with our partner that we don't even realize that our relationship is unhealthy. If you're concerned that your relationship might be unhealthy, ask yourself the following questions:

1. Are we constantly fighting?

If you and your partner are constantly fighting, it's a sign that things are not healthy. Constant arguing can lead to resentment and bitterness and can eventually destroy the relationship altogether.

2. Do we avoid talking about difficult topics?

If you and your partner avoid talking about difficult topics, it's a sign that you're not comfortable communicating with each other. When couples avoid difficult topics of conversation, they're unable to work through their problems.

If your relationship is healthy, both you and your partner should feel comfortable talking about the good things in your relationship, as well as the bad. Ideally, when couples have a concern or a problem that needs solving, they can talk it out together. When one person feels like they can't talk to their partner about certain things, it's a sign that there are bigger issues at hand.

During arguments, do you or your partner:
- Call each other names?
- Throw objects at one another?
- Punch walls, kick doors or throw things to express anger?

If so, it's a sign that the relationship is unhealthy. During an argument with my husband during our first few years of marriage, he got so angry he started punching walls. Needless to say, that wasn't a healthy way to deal with anger, and it only made things worse.

If you or your partner resort to physical violence during an argument, it's time to seek help from a professional. Physical violence is never the answer and can only lead to further damage in the relationship.

- *Blame each other for everything?*

If you and your partner constantly blame each other for everything, it's a sign that things are not healthy. When couples start to blame each other for every little thing that goes wrong in the relationship, it creates an atmosphere of distrust and resentment.
- *Shut down or walk away during arguments?*

If you and your partner shut down or walk away from each other during arguments, it's a sign that things are not healthy. Couples should be able to express their opinions without fear of becoming verbally attacked.

3. Do we have different interests?

If you and your partner no longer share the same interests, it's a sign that things might be changing in your relationship. When couples stop sharing common interests, they can start to feel like they're growing apart.

It's important to maintain some common interests, so you and your partner can continue to connect with each other. The good news is, even if you both enjoy different things, there are still ways to foster common interests together.

If your relationship is healthy, you and your partner should be able to talk about anything with each other without feeling judged. If one of you feels like the other doesn't understand, it may be a sign that the relationship is not healthy.
- *Feel like you can't talk to your partner?*

If you feel like you can't talk to your partner about certain things, it's a sign that the relationship may be unhealthy. If one of you feels uncomfortable talking to the other about anything - including money, sex or even daily life - then it may indicate that there's something wrong in the relationship.
- *Feel like your partner doesn't understand you?*

If you feel like your partner doesn't understand anything about you, it can be a sign that things are unhealthy. Even if your partner tries to listen and understand, if they're unable to do so, it may indicate a larger issue in the relationship.

4. Do we have different goals?

If you and your partner start to have different goals, it can be a sign that things are changing in the relationship. When couples no longer share common goals, they can start to feel like they're on two different paths.

It's important for couples to maintain some common ground so they can continue working together towards a shared future.
- *Have different ideas about money?*

If you and your partner have different ideas about how to handle finances, it may indicate that there's a problem in the relationship. When couples don't agree on how to spend or save money, it can lead to arguments and resentment over time.

- *Do we want children?* If you and your partner have different ideas about whether or not to have children, it can create tension in the relationship. When couples disagree about something as big as having kids, it can be difficult to continue moving forward together.
- *Do we want a future together?*

If you and your partner no longer see a future for yourselves together, it might be a sign that things are changing in the relationship. When couples no longer envision themselves together long-term, it can create tension and resentment over time.

5. Are we ready to commit?

If you and your partner are no longer committed to each other, it might be a sign that things are changing in the relationship. When couples stop feeling committed to one another, they can start drifting apart.
It's important for couples to maintain some common ground so they can continue working together towards a shared future.
- *Do we want children?* If you and your partner have different ideas about whether or not to have children, it can create tension in the relationship. When couples disagree about something as big as having kids, it can be difficult to continue moving forward together.
- *Do we want a future together?*

If you and your partner no longer see a future for yourselves together, it might be a sign that things are changing in the relationship. When couples no longer envision themselves together long-term, it can create tension and resentment over time.
It can be easy for relationships to become toxic, but it doesn't have to stay that way. In this section, we've talked about common habits of unhealthy relationships and how you can change them into a more loving relationship. One of the most important things you should do is foster some common interests with your partner, so both parties feel like they're connecting on an equal level. If things are feeling off in your relationship or if one of you feels uncomfortable talking to the other about anything, there might be a larger issue going on - which may require professional help. It's also important not only to maintain common ground when couples disagree on something as big as having children or whether or not to have kids but also to avoid drifting apart by being committed to having a future with your partner.
- *Communicate openly and honestly*

When in doubt, talk it out! One of the most crucial parts of every relationship is communication. If you feel like something's wrong, or if there's an issue that you need to bring up, communicating openly and honestly is key. Bottling things up will only make things worse in the long run.

CHAPTER 4

5 DISAGREEMENTS THAT HAPPY COUPLES HANDLE DIFFERENTLY

Couples fight. It's natural. But how you deal with those fights can make or break your relationship.
If you're tired of getting into the same arguments over and over again, try using these tips for happy couples.
These tips will help you resolve disagreements in a more positive way, so you can focus on enjoying your relationship instead of fighting about it.
Happy couples don't always agree, but they know how to deal with their disagreements in a constructive way.
Here are five distinct ways that happy couples deal with disagreements:

They communicate effectively.

Happy couples communicate effectively by listening to each other and trying to understand where the other person is coming from. They avoid defensive communication tactics like blaming, judging, and attacking.

They compromise.

Happy couples are willing to compromise in order to maintain a healthy relationship. They know that it's not about always getting their own way but about finding a middle ground that works for both of them.

They have empathy.

Happy couples have empathy for each other. They understand that each person is coming from a different place, and they are able to put themselves in their partner's shoes.

They let things go.

Happy couples don't hold grudges or bring up past mistakes during arguments. They stay focused on the issue at hand and try not to get side-tracked by old issues that have already been resolved.

They use positive reinforcement.

Happy couples use positive reinforcement to build up their partner instead of tearing them down. They complement each other, give each other support, and make sure they feel loved and appreciated.

If you want your relationship to be happy and healthy, try implementing these five habits into your own relationship. It may take a little bit of work, but it will pay off in the end!

CHAPTER 5

HOW TO BUILD HEALTHY RELATIONSHIP HABITS

FOR YOUNGER COUPLE

It's never too late to build healthy relationship habits for young couples. It's never too late to learn how to have a healthy, happy relationship, even if you've been in a horrible relationship for years. In fact, developing healthy relationship practices can help you avoid problems in the future.

If you're in a young relationship, here are some tips for building healthy relationship habits:

Talk openly and honestly. One of the best ways to build a strong foundation for your relationship is to talk openly and honestly with each other. Share your thoughts and feelings, and be willing to listen to what your partner has to say.

Be Honest

The most important habit for any relationship is honesty. You have to be able to trust each other and be honest with each other about your feelings, thoughts, and needs. If you can't be honest, then the relationship will never work.

Listen to Each Other

Listening is also key in a healthy relationship. You need to be able to listen to your partner and understand what they're saying. Don't just wait for your turn to talk; actually, listen to them. This will help build a strong connection with your partner.

Resolve Conflict Quickly

Conflict is inevitable in any relationship, but it's how you handle that conflict that matters. If you let it drag on for too long, then the relationship will eventually fall apart. The best way to resolve conflict is to address it as soon as possible and come up with a solution together.

Communication Skills, Communication Habits, Healthy Relationship Tips

Show Affection & Love Each Other Regularly

Another one of the most important habits to have in a relationship is showing affection and love for your partner. You need to show that you care about them, not just when they're around but also when they aren't with you. Showing affection and love will help build trust in the relationship.

Be Supportive Of Each Other's Dreams & Goals

You both have dreams and goals, and it's important to be supportive of each other. If you want your partner to achieve their dreams, then you need to support them in any way possible.

Be Positive & Encouraging To Each Other

You also need to be positive and encouraging towards each other. The best way to do this is through actions like giving compliments, telling your partner that you're proud of them, and just being overall positive towards them.

Make Time For Each Other

Last but not least, one of the most important habits to have in a relationship is making time for each other. You need to be able to put your partner first and make time for them in your Schedule. This can be difficult with busy lives, but it's important to find time for each other.

Building healthy relationship habits can seem daunting, but if you start with these eight habits, you're on the right track. It will take time and effort, but eventually, your relationship will be stronger than ever.

The relationship is an important aspect of a person's life. It is necessary to take care of it so that the couple can live a happy and relaxed life. The following are unhealthy relationship habits that must be avoided in order for the relationship to blossom:

Frequent arguments without any resolution- this will only lead to resentment and frustration on both parts, not to mention that it's really exhausting.

Keeping secrets from each other- can lead to a lack of trust and distrust between the partners. It has been observed that keeping secrets often leads to a breakup because there is no communication anymore between them, which then results in misunderstanding one another's needs and wants.

CHAPTER 6

HOW TO BUILD HEALTHY RELATIONSHIP HABITS

FOR OLDER COUPLE

Great connections don't happen by accident. In truth, it takes years of practice—and a slew of blunders—to create the kind of marriage that appears to be effortless on the surface. However, the longer you've been together, the simpler it is to take your partner for granted, and the things you used to do to keep your relationship healthy and passionate tend to go away.

What's the good news? There's always time to turn things around, no matter how old you are or how long you've been married. We've compiled a list of simple strategies to be a better spouse beyond 40 with the advice of relationship experts.

1. Make yourself more open

It's rarely pleasant or simple to genuinely express your vulnerability in front of your partner, no matter how long you've been together. However, doing so is an important part of maintaining a healthy relationship.

"Being sensitive, honest, and understanding with your relationship involves maintaining healthy communication," explains Babita Spinelli, founder of Opening the Doors Psychotherapy. "Closing any gaps in communication that have been established makes for a better spouse."

2. Stay in touch with each other throughout the day.

You and your spouse may be able to go hours, if not days, without checking in if you both have busy schedules or travel frequently. However, if you want to strengthen your relationship after 40, you should stick to a routine of regular check-ins.

"Everyone gets busy," says therapist Jessica Marchena, LMHC, "but a quick text or call to your spouse doesn't take much time." "It's critical for the health of your marriage because it demonstrates that you care about and consider your partner."

3 You should indeed sleep in the same bed.

Your partner's constant snoring or blanket-hogging may have prompted you to seek greener pastures—most likely the couch—a long time ago. However, if you want your relationship to be more stable in the future, you must get back into the same bed. "Please see your doctor and figure out a solution to these problems," Marchena advises, "because sleeping together in the same bed is crucial for the health of your marriage." She also claims that sleeping in the same room strengthens not only a couple's physical bond but also their emotional bond. If your relationship isn't moving forward,

4 At around the same time, go to bed.

You're missing out on important moments of contact and intimacy if you and your partner have different sleep schedules—one of you is already fast asleep by the time the other comes to bed. According to a 2015 Warren Evans study covered by The Daily Mail, a shocking 75% of couples admit to going to bed at different times and missing out on those moments.

5 Ask for what you want but keep in mind that you may not always get it.

There's no better time than now to learn to accept that things don't always go your way if you want to be a better spouse. Don't be afraid to express your needs, but keep in mind that your partner can't—and won't—always fulfill them.

6 Choose your battles wisely.

While you may have entered your relationship with rose-colored glasses, you will become more aware of the things they do that irritate you after some time together. However, if you want your relationship to stay on solid ground, you should make a conscious decision about which issues you believe are important to discuss with them and which you should let slide.

7 Make forgiveness a habit.

Nobody is perfect, including your spouse, but if you want to keep your marriage together, you must occasionally forgive their flaws.
"Accept that your spouse is doing the best he or she can given the circumstances at the time," Sultanoff says, advising forgiving them for honest mistakes and moving on rather than dwelling on perceived errors.

8. Don't be so adamant about compromising all of the time.

While many people believe that compromise is the key to a successful and healthy relationship, it can also mean that neither party gets exactly what they want or, more significantly, need. Accept that not every issue will have a completely equitable conclusion rather than always attempting to meet in the middle.

9 Be aware of the signals you're sending.

According to Chelsea Hudson, LCPC, of Cityscape Counselling, even when you are plainly stating one thing to your partner, your body language may be sending a completely other impression.

"While you may say 'I'm fine' or 'thank you,' your tone and facial movements may indicate otherwise," Hudson adds. She recommends speaking honestly and checking yourself in the mirror to make sure your facial expressions reflect what you're saying to avoid this.

10 Don't expect anything in return when you give.

In many relationships, everyday actions can take on a quid pro quo quality — "I prepared dinner, so you clean up; I put the kids to bed, so I can go out with my friends," and so forth. Acts of kindness, on the other hand, should not be so transactional, which is why it's crucial to put forth effort even if you don't know if you'll be rewarded.

CHAPTER 7

HOW BEST TO BUILD HEALTHY RELATIONSHIP HABITS FOR SAME-SEX COUPLE

Is heterosexual dating the same as same-sex dating? Both yes and no.
Anyone seeking a long-term, committed relationship has similar difficulties. However, as a member of the LGBTQ community, you have certain needs and concerns.
Discrimination may occur at home, school, or at employment. The severity of these traumatic experiences varies, but they can have an impact on one's sense of self-worth and self-esteem. As a result, your dating and relationship life may be affected.
There are new possibilities.
New same-sex marriage legislation, as well as a more progressive society, have made it easier for LGBTQ people to marry, have children, and start families. They've also given the community a new perspective on commitments and families.
Despite these advancements, same-sex couples still face hurdles. Unlike heterosexual relationships, which have historically followed a well-defined road to marriage, same-sex couples have few models to follow. It's difficult to know what to do next without advice or role models, whether you want to get married or not.

The difficulties

LGBTQ folks suffer many of the same obstacles as their heterosexual counterparts in many respects. Finding a compatible mate, forming a solid, long-lasting relationship, and improving that relationship over time all need the same amount of effort.
Coming out and the reality of oppression, on the other hand, have a direct and tangible impact on LGBTQ people. This could have an impact on how you search for and find a compatible match.
The internet's and social media's ascent
The availability of the Internet and mobile apps has drastically altered how people discover romantic companions. Bars, restaurants, and other social areas where same-sex couples would ordinarily meet have been supplanted by dating services and apps.

LGBTQ partnership rates have risen considerably in recent decades as finding a partner has become easier. More than 60% of same-sex couples meet online, according to studies, and there are more gay and lesbian couples than ever before.

However, online dating has impacted how people make relationship decisions. People may be less attentive to more suitable mates and more vulnerable to connecting with mismatched partners as a result of the abundance of options. This is especially true for people looking for a long-term partner.

There is an excessive amount of choice.

Furthermore, the illusion of limitless possibility and choice may lead people to abandon a good relationship if it does not immediately satisfy the majority of their wants. Why bother if there's something better out there already?

This perspective, however, isn't totally correct. We want our partners to be our greatest friends, satisfy all of our sexual fantasies and needs, support our aspirations, share our financial responsibilities, and accept all of our imperfections, which makes dating difficult. Relationships, on the other hand, necessitate work and ongoing maintenance. Conflicts over differences may develop as the romantic part of a relationship gives way to the following stage, as they do in any relationship. That isn't to say it isn't worth giving a shot.

What role does oppression have in dating?

People in the LGBTQ community face a significant risk of stigmatization, discrimination, marginalization, and violence as a sexual minority. They are sometimes victimized by their own parents, siblings, and other close relatives.

Internalization of oppression is possible. Shame, self-hatred, and self-deprecating behavior result. As a result, it may have an impact on eating habits. Some members of the LGBTQ community may have a proclivity to repeat rejection and blame patterns or to stay in a toxic relationship for an extended period of time.

Coming out of the closet

Coming out might have an impact on dating. Dating difficulties vary depending on when a person began the process of coming out. The more recently a person has come out, the more anxious he or she will be when dating.

Each person's experiences with being "out" to family, friends, and the workplace are unique. Some individuals may know you're out, while others may not. This can lead to emotions of worry, melancholy, and shame, especially if you're dating someone who is still in the process of coming out.

LGBTQ people of color

You may be subjected to numerous levels of oppression if you identify as a member of an ethnic minority. Furthermore, research reveals that discrimination against homosexual men and lesbian women from ethnic minorities can come from inside their own families. Many LGBTQ people of color hide their same-sex dating activities and may live a double life due to cultural beliefs and a fear of embarrassing their relatives. It may be more difficult to date in these conditions.

Tips for Having a Successful Same-Sex Relationship

Love may endure despite the difficulties. You can find a long-term relationship with the proper attitude and the correct skills.

1. Seek advice from a dating coach or a counselor if you've been out of the dating environment for a long period. You can look for same-sex dating advice on the internet. Because first dates can be nerve-wracking, it's a good idea to do your homework and be prepared.

2. Date someone who is going through a similar transition. A relationship's future success is more likely if both partners are at or near the same stage. You may grow dissatisfied and resentful of your partner if you are out and he or she is not. This is due to his or her reluctance to be open and honest about the relationship. On the other hand, the pair's more secretive members may feel compelled to come out before he or she is emotionally ready. This might also contribute to feelings of anxiousness and resentment.

3. Rethink your connection with social media if you're hoping for a long-term relationship rather than a hookup. Many social networking platforms are not conducive to love and commitment. Instead, they concentrate on the culture of hookups. This may have an impact on how your dates see you.

4. Be clear about your monogamy and nonmonogamy principles and express them openly. Make your implicit expectations explicit by clarifying them. Don't assume that your partner's definition of infidelity is the same as yours. Encourage your sexual tastes and expectations to be discussed. If you want to be in a long-term, committed relationship, and you want to be loyal and monogamous, look for someone who shares your beliefs. These tough conversations can be facilitated by a well-trained sex therapist.

5. Don't rush into a relationship. We sometimes make decisions regarding living together without truly thinking about it. It's unavoidable. Many same-sex and LGBTQ couples say they moved in together because their lease was up for renewal or because they already spent a lot of nights together. Living together is both an emotional and a financial decision. It is not something that should be done on the spur of the moment.

6. seek relationship counseling if you've had terrible experiences coming out if you've been discriminated against in your family, school, or workplace, or if you don't have much support right now. Those experiences can have a negative impact on your self-esteem. In your dating life, you may see that you keep repeating the same patterns. Seek counseling to unlock your potential and strengthen your resilience in order to increase your chances of having a successful same-sex relationship.

Finally, remember that what makes LGBTQ relationships successful are the same elements that make any relationship succeed: focus on the relationship, a healthy sex life, kindness, respect, communication, compromise, trust, and safety. To get on the right track, seek the advice of a dating and relationship specialist.

CHAPTER 8

9 NEW WAYS TO STRENGTHEN YOUR BOND IN YOUR RELATIONSHIP

It shouldn't be difficult to have a happy relationship! That's one of the encouraging results of my landmark marriage study, which has followed 373 married couples since 1983.

Here's some more great news for lovers: If you're in a good relationship, whether married or not, you can keep it that way or improve it by adopting a few new behaviors and tiny modifications. While many relationship experts advise focusing on what's wrong with the relationship, my research reveals that adding good behaviors to the partnership has a considerably higher influence on couples' happiness.

Based on my research, here are nine strategies to strengthen your relationship link and be a happier pair.

1. Recognize and respect your partner's individuality. We've all had fantasies about our lover being thinner, wealthier, more romantic, and so on. Examine your expectations and see how reasonable they are. Unrealistic expectations lead to persistent frustration, which is the primary cause of relationship failure, according to my research.

2. Perform random acts of kindness on a regular basis. Small gestures that communicate "I'm thinking of you" are crucial in maintaining a strong relationship tie — for example, he fills up her gas tank, and she gives him a steaming cup of coffee in bed. Small gestures of affection include hand-holding, touching, and sending a love email in the middle of the day. The accumulation of tiny gestures has a greater influence on partner pleasure than grand, less frequent actions, according to research.

3. Set aside 10 minutes each day to connect with others. Most couples believe they communicate with one another all of the time. But how often do you discuss topics that allow you to gain a better knowledge of your partner? The happy couples in my study talked to each other regularly about things other than their relationship, and they felt they understood a lot about their partner in four crucial areas: friends, stressors, life dreams, and values. Set aside 10 minutes a day to talk to your partner about anything other than a job, family, the house, or the relationship — I call it "The 10-Minute Rule." This small adjustment breathes new energy into relationships.

4. Fall in love with yourself all over again on a weekly basis.

While spontaneous dates are fun, the truth is that we're all too busy to devote time to our partners. Keep your love relationship healthy by going out once a week for dinner, a movie, dancing, seeing an art exhibit, or doing couples yoga. Take it in turns to plan it. Men: studies suggest that when women are away from their children and duties, they are more passionate, and their libido is stronger. Check out what happens when you reserve a night at a nearby hotel and enlist the help of a friend or relative to look after the kids and pets.

5. Change and evolve as a team.

Your love relationship is a living organism that needs sustenance in order to thrive. Infusing it with change is the best approach to foster it. Introducing change into relationships has been found to be a critical factor in pair satisfaction, similar to fertilizer for a plant. The adjustments can be minor, but they must cause enough disruption in his or her routine to cause him or her to sit up and take notice. Change roles: Allow her to make the dinner reservation if he always does. Alternatively, break up routines by taking a day off from work and doing something interesting with your friends, such as visiting a museum or a nearby tourist attraction. Try something new: go on a meditation retreat or take a water-skiing class together.

6. Become acquainted with each other's acquaintances and family.

Men, in particular, are happier when the female has a solid relationship with his family, according to my research. Couples who accept, but do not necessarily love, each other's friends and make an attempt to get to know their report being happier than couples who have distinct social circles and families.

7. Volunteer as a caregiver.

Support is one of the three things that couples require in order to have a good relationship (the other two needs are reassurance and intimacy). One of the most crucial parts of a great relationship, according to the happy couples in my survey, is having a partner who is "there for them." Instrumental help, or support that fixes or solves a problem, is something that many men enjoy doing. Women enjoy providing emotional support in the form of empathic listening and constructive criticism. First, figure out what kind of assistance your partner actually wants, and then give it to him or her on a regular basis.

8. Keep things light — and bright.

Laughter is a form of spirituality. It functions as happy medicine in marriage. To avoid your relationship from becoming stagnant, you must strike a balance between the sensible and the enjoyable components of your connection. Yes, you must take specific steps to maintain order in your life and the stability of your relationship. However, don't forget to have fun. Attempt to regain the pure joy of playing a game, behaving childishly in the snow, watching a stupid movie, dragging her onto the dance floor, and so on.

9. Find a healthy communication method.

In my long-term study of marriage, the happy couples all reported that solid communication skills were what kept them together and thriving. This entails not only asking your spouse what he or she requires but also telling them what you require. It means checking in on a regular basis to see what pressures are surfacing in your partner's life and learning how to fight fairly — no name-calling, humiliating, or bringing up everything that has annoyed you in the previous year.

CHAPTER 9

10 OLD SCHOOL RELATIONSHIP HABITS THAT SHOULD BE REINTRODUCED

Is it just me, or are there more of us who have a strong desire to go back in time when it comes to eating habits?

This hookup culture may be exhausting at times, and I often wonder if there are still men out there who are ready to go out of their way to impress a woman.

Some old-school dating traditions should undoubtedly make a comeback — or at the very least, their spirit should be preserved and modernized.

This is how everything should look:

1. A man who asks a woman out on a date several days in advance

I'm not suggesting there's anything wrong with a woman taking the initiative, but I think the whole dating experience is better when the male goes out of his way to show real interest.

These days, a man who takes his time and plans a date is extremely rare. We frequently only receive last-minute plans and late-night phone calls to hang out, which is very disappointing.

2. Clearly stating your aims from the start

This is unquestionably one of the greatest aspects of traditional dating practices. When you were going steady with someone, or as we used to say, 'exclusive,' you knew it. There wasn't much of a fuss when it came to having 'the conversation.' You would simply ask someone if they wanted to be with you — well, guys normally did since it was a macho thing to do, even if there were some exceptions back then.

3. Making an effort to look your best

"You never have a second chance to create a first impression," as the saying goes. That is correct. Before we get to know the soul of the person we're dating, we need something to draw us in.

It's nice when both men and women put forth the effort to dress nicely, smell nice, and make someone aware that they are trying to impress them. Efforts are seductive.

4. Slow-motion dance

You don't get much of a chance to slow dance these days when you go clubbing. Because the music is so loud, you can't hear each other.

Fortunately, there are still some places where you can slow dance, and you should take advantage of that opportunity. Even if you're not a great dancer, it's a chance to learn something new with your friends.

The sound of music and a relaxed setting relaxes both men and women, allowing them to converse more freely. It also puts them in close physical proximity, which heightens the sexual tension between them.

5. A modernized version of proper etiquette

Even though opening car doors (or any doors) for a woman, giving her a flower when you go out on a date, pulling out her chair, or something similar sounds great and should never go out of style, most people these days would find it awkward.

But why can't we simply modernize and bring some things up to date? Allowing a woman to order first, walking beside her holding her hand instead of a few steps ahead of her, sending a goodnight text, and so on are examples of polished manners these days.

6. Assisting a lady to her front door

It's not just about being polite. It's chivalry on a one-on-one basis, and it should never go out of style. First and foremost, it's a fantastic kissing opportunity that smells of passion in our less-than-romantic modern period.

Second, it gives a lady a sense of security. It sends the message that the man is concerned about the woman's safety on a subconscious level, which we could all use more of these days.

7. Making a romantic gesture of grandeur

It may be wishful thinking, but wouldn't it be lovely if someone did something extraordinary for you? As if it were a genuine love letter, a poem, or perhaps a serenade performed beneath your window.

Perhaps bringing you a cup of coffee in the morning, leaving cute post-its with love sayings all over the flat, and hiding chocolate in your purse are more appropriate today. Any female would be knocked off her feet by these little large objects.

8. There is no access to the internet.

Unplugging is beneficial from time to time. Our phones take up a lot of our time and attention. We don't pay attention to half of what the other person has to say.

That's why it'd be fantastic if two people on a date turned off their wi-fi (or at the very least avoided checking their phone every 5 seconds) and simply talked to each other like they used to.

9. Establishing a relationship gradually

This is something that should surely be done these days, and we'd all have a higher chance of finding love. We become impatient and skip over the processes that lead to a relationship, hoping for the best.

The old school method had its own tempo, which was slower but of higher quality. It wasn't necessary to hasten anything. They relished the experience and turned courting into an art form.

10. Rather than giving up, try to fix things.
In old-school dating, this is a critical stage. People had a very different perspective back then. They weren't quitters; they were fixers. They were eager to work together to solve difficulties and actually listen to one another.
Relationships required time and investment back then, as they do now, but love was always worth the effort and investment.
That's probably why their marriages endured, and they were able to spend their golden years with someone they loved.

CHAPTER 10

15 PRACTICES FOR COUPLES TO STEER A TOXIC RELATIONSHIP INTO A MORE LOVING, RELAXED, HAPPY, CLOSE AND ENJOYING RELATIONSHIP STARTING FROM TODAY.

You've probably met at least one of those 'perfect couples,' the ones you can't picture ever breaking up or even bickering. They're absolutely content and totally committed to each other, whether they've been together for 40 years, 20 years, or even just a year or two. Have you ever pondered how they were able to create such a perfect balance and happiness? Of course, every marriage is unique, but here are five things those couples are likely to have done, and continue to do.

1. Emphasize the positive

People in pleasant, successful relationships recognize that excessive criticism harms their partner's self-worth and leads to resentment.
If you want to keep your relationship happy, criticize as little as possible, if at all possible. Instead, focus on your partner's positive qualities by delivering regular and substantial compliments.

2. Good communication leads to good relationships.

Couples in happy relationships keep their relationships joyful by maintaining open channels of communication and conversing every day. They not only verbally encourage and reinforce each other, but they also express their affection through physical touch and set aside time in their day for intimacy.
To form a stronger link with your spouse, share your own sentiments, and sincerely listen to what he has to say when he shares his. Keep your physical bond as strong as your emotional bond by sneaking in a kiss now and then.

3. Your partner is a real, flawed person, and you should love him for it!

If all you know about how relationships function and what they should be like comes from movies, television, and books, you should expect real life to surprise, disappoint, and eventually extend your perspective.

Every relationship has its challenges. When they do, it's a major error to assume you didn't chose the appropriate individual and need to try again. Couples that have discovered true happiness have done it by loving one other for who they are.

4. Allow each other to pursue own interests.

Couples in happy, healthy relationships share common interests, but they also have unique interests, and they appreciate each other's choices. They don't always do things with each other just because they think they should.

For instance, if the couples' dance classes you're attempting to take together are producing conflicts and tension every week, go out with your friends that evening and tell your partner to do the same.

You're actually exhibiting a commitment to stay together when you take time to do things separately and give your relationship some space. Consider this: if you're always together, you'll never get a chance to look forward to seeing each other!

5. Be sure to surprise your partner every now and then.

Even if you and your spouse have been together for so long that you can recount one other's favorite stories off the top of your heads, doing something unexpected for your partner can help strengthen your bond.

Consider doing something little to break up the monotony of your daily lives, such as going to a movie during the week or simply giving each other your entire attention for a short period of time with no electronic gadgets to distract you.

6. Come to an agreement

Each person adds their own tastes, opinions, and communication strategies to any partnership. These personal characteristics may or may not coincide with those of the other, resulting in potential problems if one is unwilling to compromise or even give up some of their views. Instead of fighting, people who have extremely effective personal and professional connections reach agreements. There is an agreement in place regarding how to communicate if someone is late in meeting some kind of obligation. Of course, you can't plan for every situation or circumstance and come to an agreement. You can reflect back with the other person after a problem has developed, acknowledge what went wrong in the conversation, and agree to do something better next time.

Strong emotional reactions are often evoked when someone disagrees with you or has a different communication style than you. These emotional reactions are programmed into us from previous experiences. By employing agreements, you are deciding to change your manner because the old pattern most likely resulted in an unsatisfactory outcome. To summarize, you must be willing to examine your emotions, how you react, and be driven to improve. Understand what you're contributing and how you may improve if you want your relationships to be successful. You will be unsatisfied with the results if you put someone else in charge of changing things for you.

7. Relationships Aren't Necessary

For the sake of clarity and emphasis, I'll say it again. People in successful relationships do not require the relationship; rather, they desire it. They are not seeking for the other person to replace a previously unmet vacuum in their lives. Successful people spend time getting to know themselves, are content being alone and with others, yet they seek out relationships and connections with others because they appreciate the inherent significance of interpersonal interactions. They enter the relationship with an open mind and are prepared for anything that may arise.

When you enter a relationship looking for something in this person that wasn't present in the previous one, you're putting a chunk of your happiness in their hands. Putting your emotions and sentiments in the hands of someone else is a recipe for disappointment. Learn to be content with yourself. Work on the aspects of yourself that need to be improved, and take full responsibility for your own happiness in any relationship.

8. Don't Get Enamoured with Someone's Possibilities

In intimate connections, we frequently perceive features in someone that are endearing or attractive, even if it is only a glimpse of them. However, these traits may not be consistent or displayed in a way that we find appealing, and you're left wondering what the other would be like if he or she acted in this manner all of the time. You might think to yourself, "The relationship would be so much better, more interesting, more rewarding." Our thoughts project into the future, where all of the other's excellent features are constantly displayed, and you may believe that person has a lot of promise.

Recognizing potential is a huge step forward. It's a negative if it's the reason you're still in the relationship. The person you imagine in the future is not the person you are with right now, and there is no way of knowing whether or not this person will mature into the person you envision in the future.

Work on respecting and understanding the person you're with right now, since that's who they are now and will be in the future. You must make a decision if you are unhappy with the current person. Do you stick it out and accept that this is who they will always be, or do you cut it off and consider the prospect of someone better?

Those in successful relationships may have visions of their perfect future mate, but they are focused on the now.

9. You'd Rather Be Happy Than Accurate

Differences in opinion cause the bulk of conflicts in personal and professional interactions. You have a different ideology than the other person and attempt to convince them that you are right, or vice versa. The length of the debate or conversation is determined by how strongly one believes their beliefs are correct. The worst-case situation, which happens all too often, is that the conflict goes unresolved and the dispute is postponed.

Putting your desire to be happy above your need to be right is a key to having functional relationships. It makes no difference if you believe the other person is incorrect; it is not your obligation to prove it. It's also not your place to stand up for what you believe is correct. As one wise philosopher once put it, "You have no legal standing. It is possible for someone else to wrong you if you have rights."

Don't hand over control of your happiness to someone else. Put your happiness first, ignore your need to be right, and choose happiness instead. Conflicts will lessen as a result, and the door will open for better communication.

10. Recognize and express what makes you feel loved.

This secret is more appropriate to personal relationships, but by substituting the word 'respected' for 'loved,' it can also be applied to professional ones. What makes you feel loved, and how does someone know that? The solution is straightforward. You must first figure out what triggers that reaction before telling the person you're with. Although this appears to be a simple process, few couples actually follow it, and miscommunication around it leads to conflict.

Take, for example, your partner's sense of love as Chocolate. Your understanding, on the other hand, is that your lover feels love as Vanilla. As a result, you go out and buy vanilla ice cream in the hopes of proving your devotion. "I just want you to love me!" shouts the other, unhappy with you. Such statements elicit significant feelings from the other person, who believed they were demonstrating their love for Vanilla by making such statements. Chocolate was what the partner actually desired, and Vanilla might offend him.

Arguments arise in all relationships when one partner feels unheard and the other believes their efforts are undervalued. When one person has a strong need to prove their argument, to be correct, the conflict can quickly escalate. To avoid this, say out loud what makes you feel loved, respected, and valued, and then say it again and again. Don't count on your companion to recall. The more you repeat it, the more likely it will be remembered and implemented.

11. Tell it like it is

This is the most basic secret, and if it isn't followed, it will cause the most strife. We all want and expect others to be open and honest with us, to express their actual feelings, wants, and emotions. Furthermore, in any form of relationship, honesty is essential to having faith in the other. Logic dictates that you must reciprocate what you expect from your relationship. If you want someone to be honest with you, you must be honest with them.

Most people in relationship settings are frustrated by their partner's motives, which they doubt or distrust. People are professionals at making assumptions about the motivations behind someone's actions, often unfavorable ones. What does your mind think if your partner claims he or she will be home at 5 p.m. but isn't home by 6 p.m.? What assumptions do you make about why the other is late, the type of person he or she is, or the implications of this conduct now?

You have no means of knowing if your logical or illogical assumptions are correct unless your spouse tells you. Don't get caught up in preconceptions. Concentrate on self-controlling what you can. Be truthful in all situations, demand it in return, and let others know when you don't get it. Maintain this behavior, and others will reciprocate with honesty.

12. Come to an agreement on financial matters

Another important aspect of a happy marriage is reaching an agreement on financial matters. Financial issues may cause a lot of strife in a marriage. Both partners should become more conscious of their financial positions and create an easy-to-follow budget. This will avoid any money troubles in the marriage from becoming a source of contention.

13. Don't Bring Up Creepy Subjects

Keep topics that could cause strife in your marriage at bay. While it is completely okay to hold differing viewpoints on issues such as politics or religion, it is not acceptable to allow your differences of opinion to lead to a divorce. If you appreciate your partner and his or her opinions, you can have a happy marriage.

14. Before getting married, come to an agreement on important issues.

Before you marry, get to know your partner and talk about important matters. It would be devastating, for example, to find out after marriage that your partner does not want any children while you wish to start a family. Differences of opinion on such important issues can completely destroy a relationship. Make sure you marry someone just after you've reached an agreement on important issues like these. It will help you avoid troubles in your marriage in the future.

15. Allow a lot of space between you and your partner.

To have a happy married existence, give each other plenty of space. Spending a lot of time together can make you feel suffocated. As a result, it's just as necessary to be apart as it is to be together and converse about your shared interests. The time you spend apart not only safeguards your marriage, but it also allows each person to maintain their individuality.

CONCLUSION

Relationships of this kind don't just happen. You must put in the effort to establish a successful connection with your significant other.

There are many more significant relationship behaviors that I've observed, but they don't appear as frequently as these 14 that appear in robust relationships that don't collapse under stress or weaken in the face of adversity. The partners in these unions are aware of what they have, recognize its rarity, and do everything possible to preserve it.

These practices will assist you in taking your relationship to the next level. After all, having a good relationship is crucial to living a happy life. Love is more than a sensation; it is also a skill that can be learned.

It takes effort to keep a long-term relationship going. It necessitates action, planning, and a commitment to supporting one another through life's ups and downs. You will have stronger and more fulfilling relationships once you grasp that love is about what you give rather than what you get.

www.ingramcontent.com/pod-product-compliance
Lightning Source LLC
Chambersburg PA
CBHW080607170426
43209CB00007B/1355

v